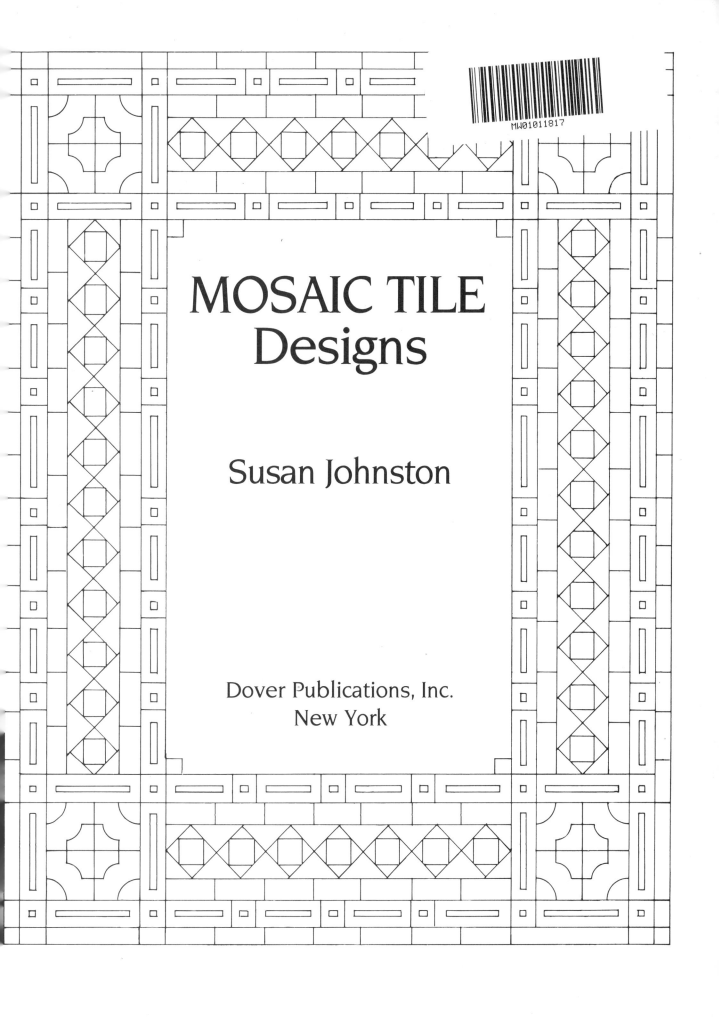

MOSAIC TILE
Designs

Susan Johnston

Dover Publications, Inc.
New York

Published in Canada by General Publishing Company, Ltd., 30 Lesmill Road, Don Mills, Toronto, Ontario.
Published in the United Kingdom by Constable and Company, Ltd., 10 Orange Street, London WC2H 7EG.

Mosaic Tile Designs, as published by Dover Publications, Inc., in 1984, is a republication of the work originally published by Dover in 1981 under the title *Mosaic Tile Coloring Book*.

DOVER *Pictorial Archive* SERIES

Mosaic Tile Designs belongs to the Dover Pictorial Archive Series. Up to ten illustrations from it may be used in any one single publication without payment to or permission from the publisher. Wherever possible include a credit line, indicating title, author and publisher. Please address the publisher for permission to make more extensive use of illustrations in this volume than that authorized above.
The reproduction of this book in whole is prohibited.

International Standard Book Number: 0-486-24080-0

Manufactured in the United States of America
Dover Publications, Inc.
180 Varick Street
New York, N.Y. 10014

1

2

4

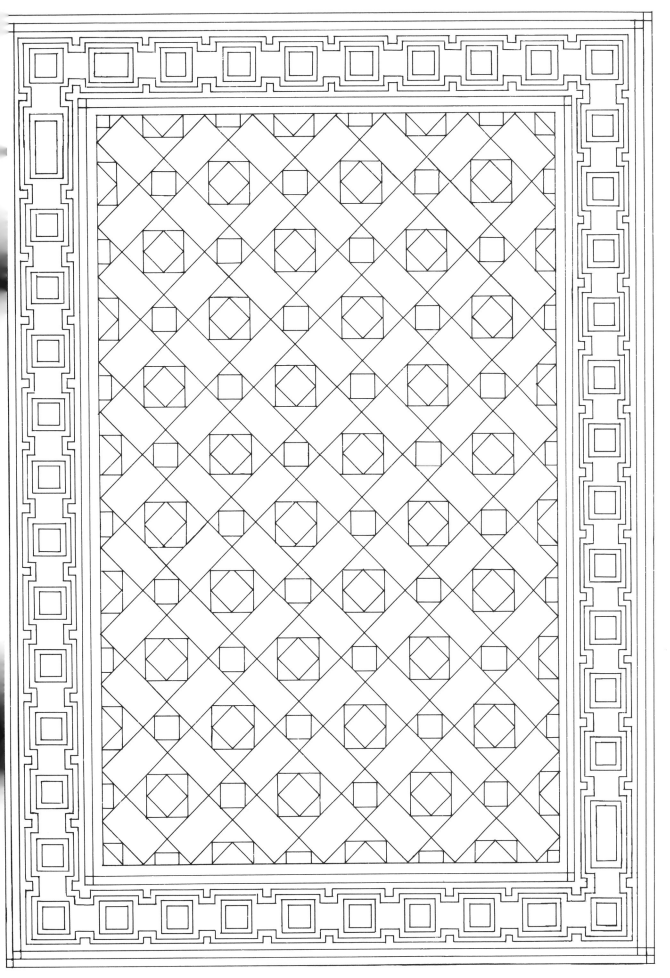

5

6

7

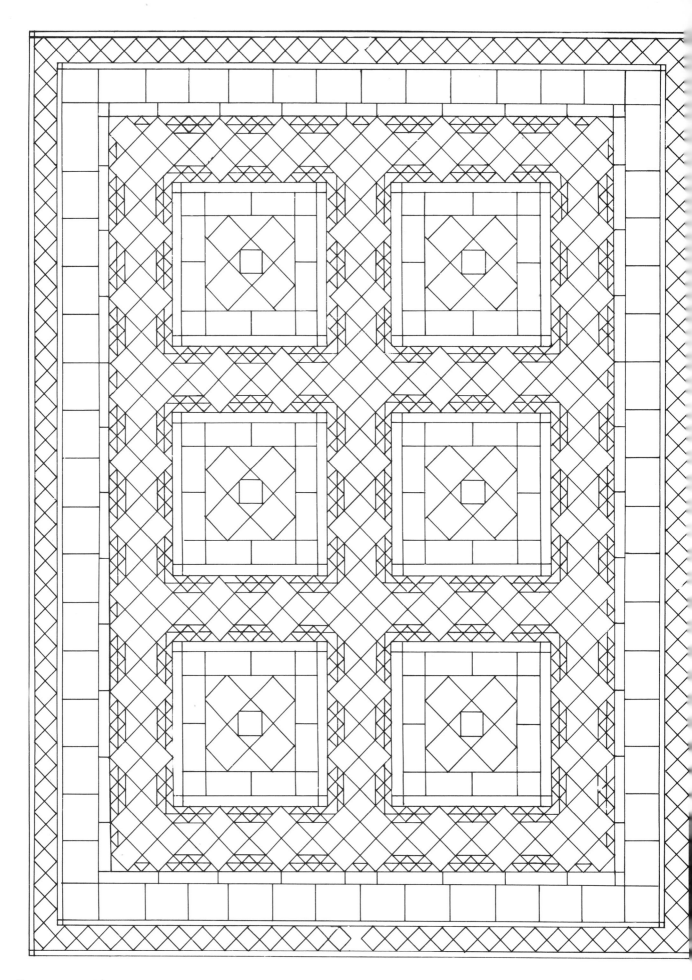

8

9

10

11

13

14

15

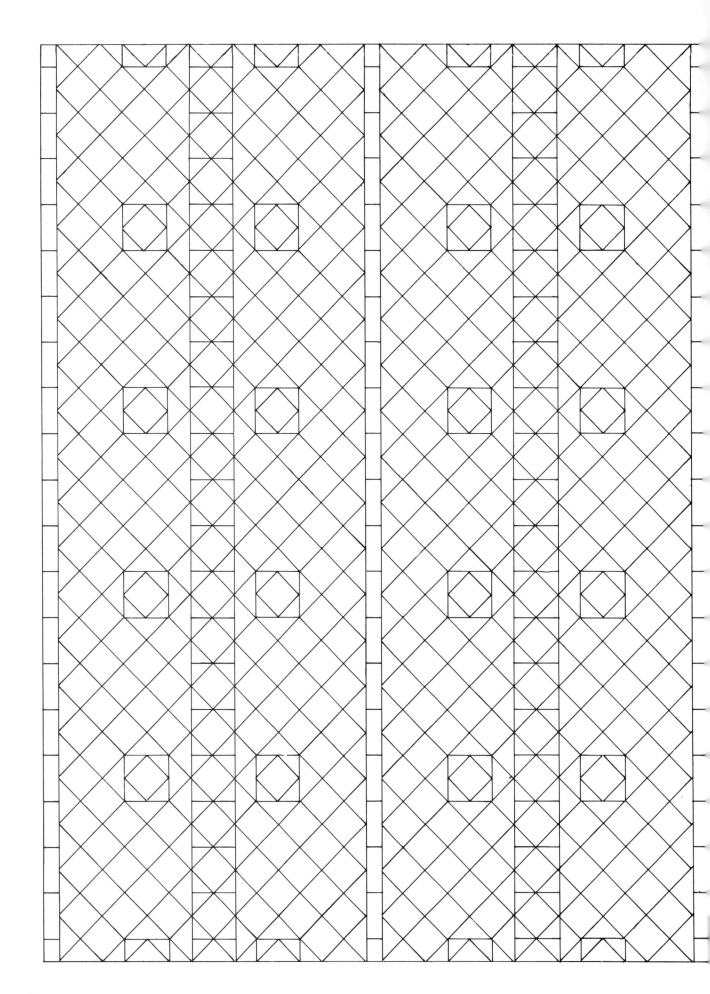

16

17

18

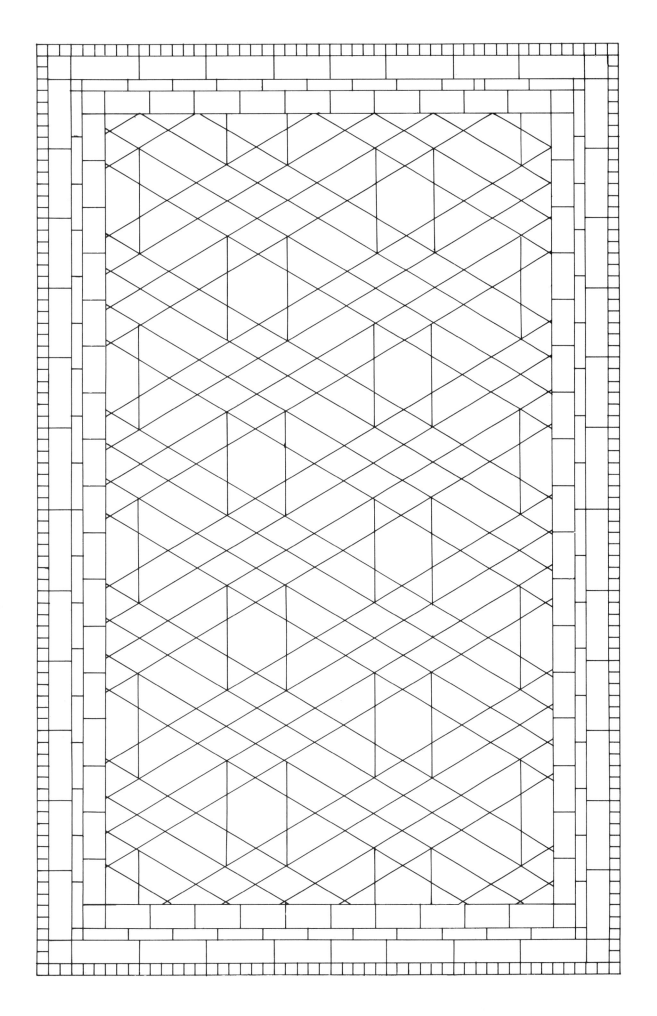

19

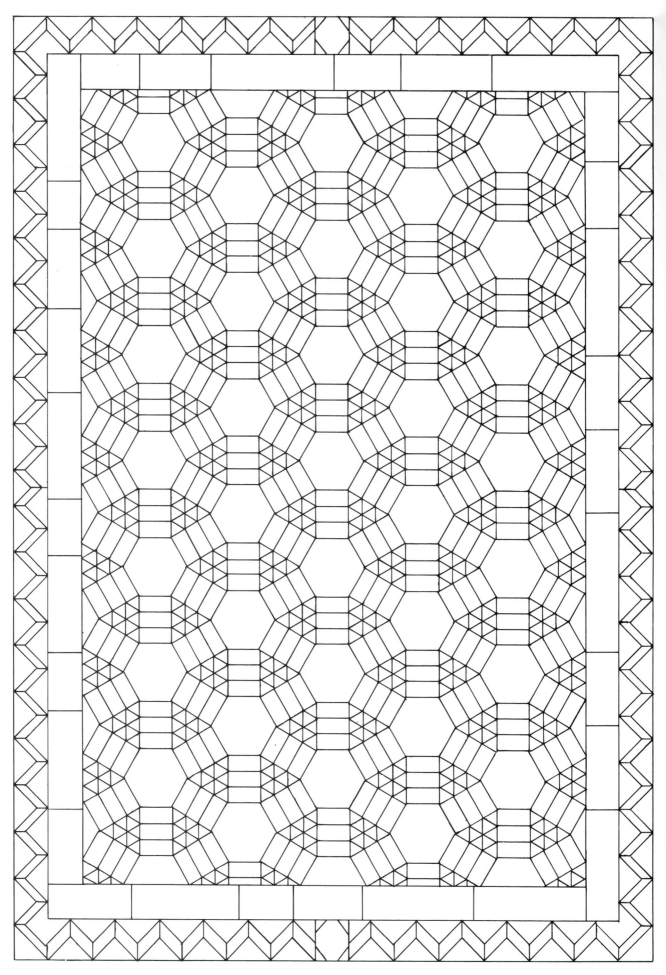

20

21

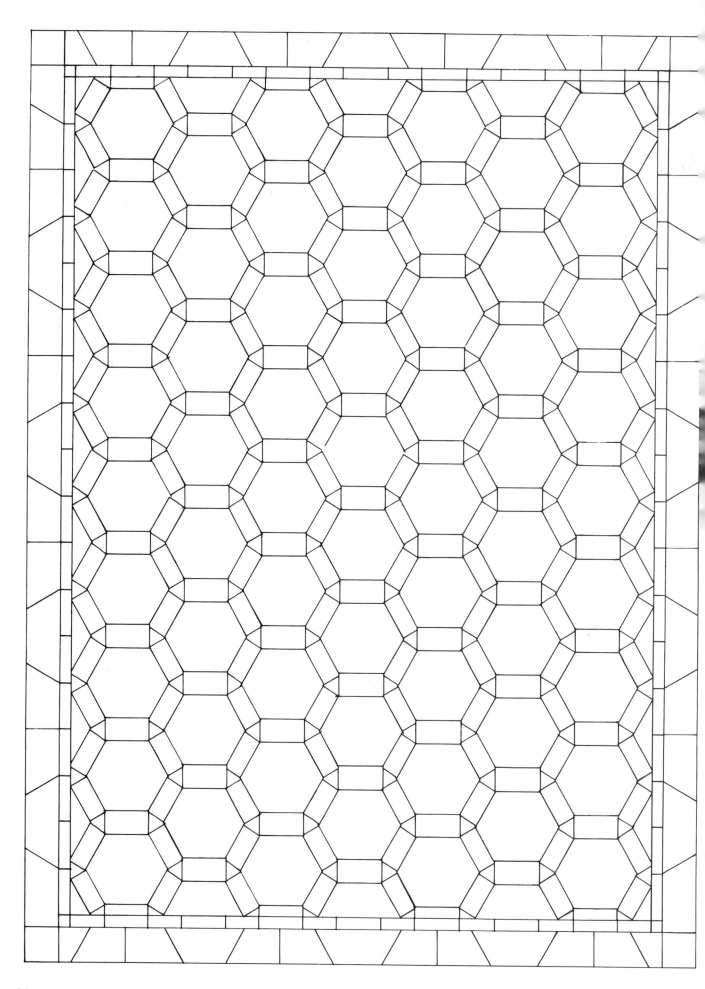

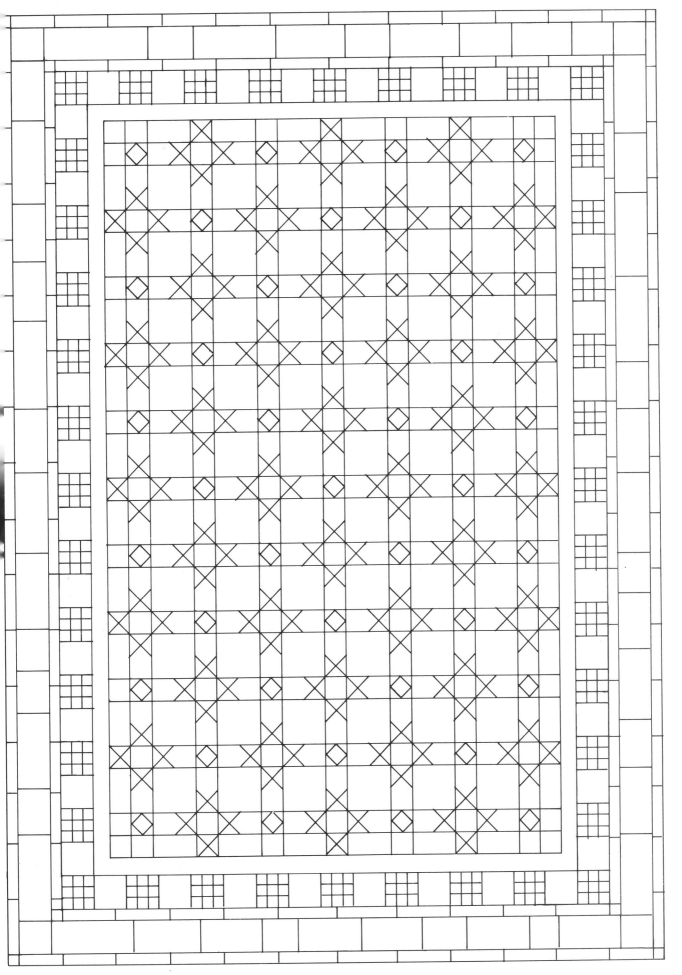

23

24

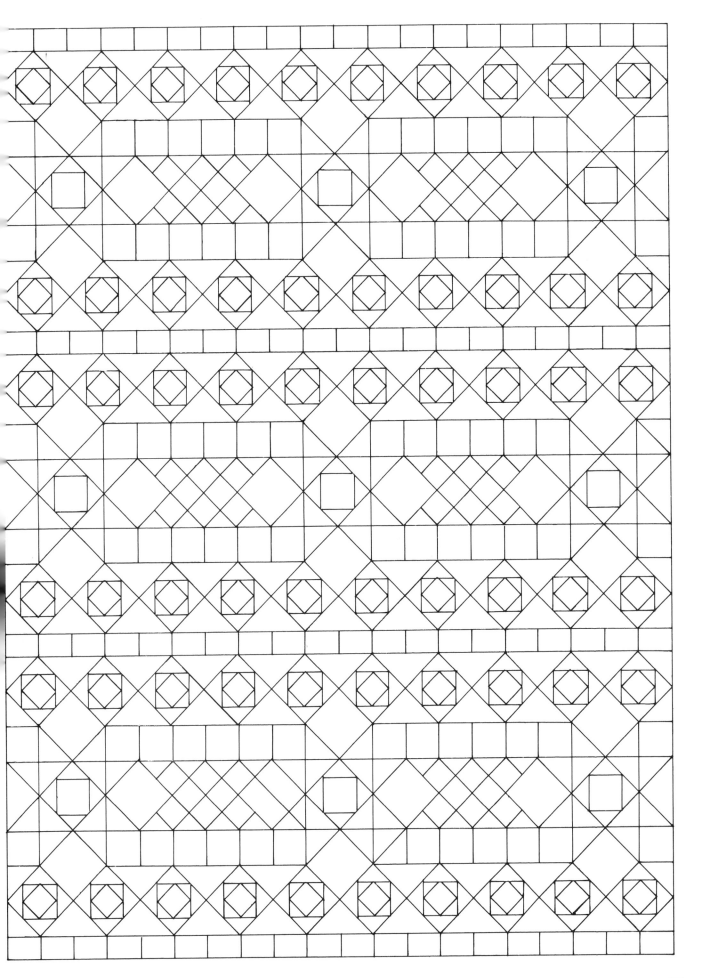

25

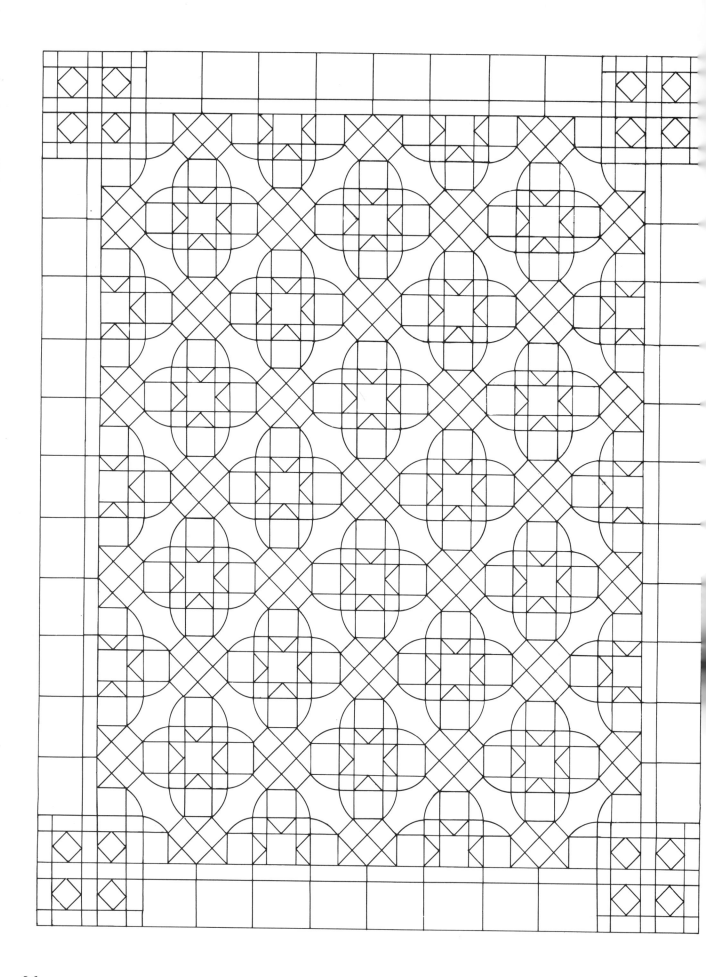

26

28

29

30

31

32

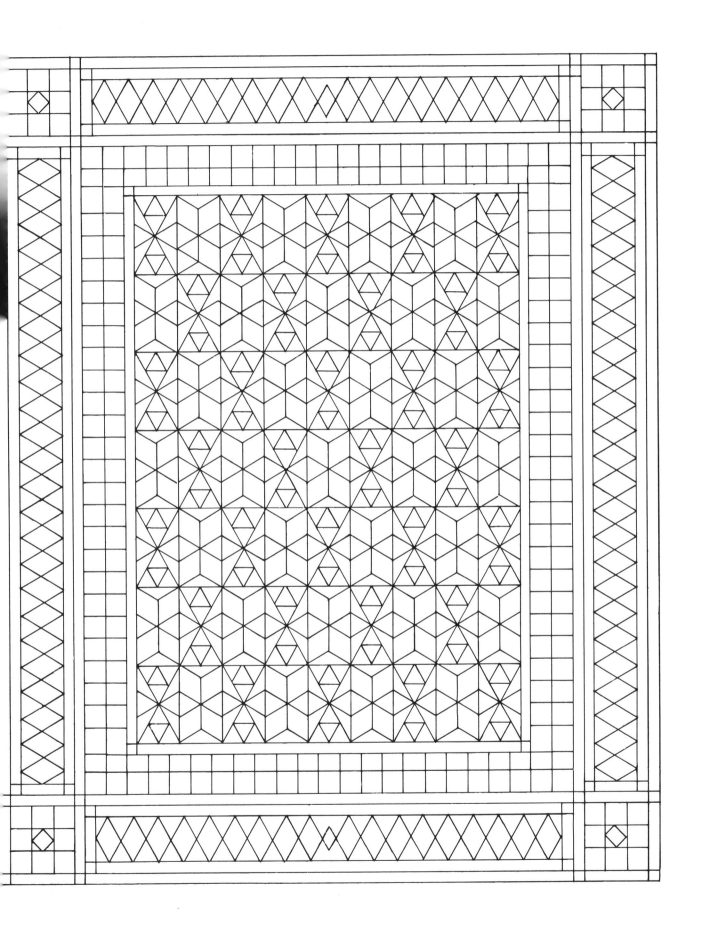

33

34

35

38

40

41

42

43

44